NOT A SILENT NIGHT
*John Gohorry*

\*

KEINE STILLE NACHT
*Bettine Koch*

# *Not a Silent Night* * John Gohorry

TRANSLATED FROM

# *Keine Stille Nacht* * Bettine Koch

Text © Bettine Koch and John Gohorry 2017

Images © Bettine Koch

ISBN 978-1-910323-99-1

Designed and typeset by Gerry Cambridge
gerry.cambridge@btinternet.com
www.gerrycambridge.com

Printed by Imprint Digital, Exeter
www.imprint.co.uk

Published by Shoestring Press
19 Devonshire Avenue, Beeston, Nottinghamshire, NG9 1BS
(0115) 925 1827
www.shoestringpress.co.uk

# Bettine Koch's poem *Keine Stille Nacht* and my rendering of it as *Not a Silent Night*

In April 2008, Bettine Koch, an old friend from Stuttgart, read me the German original of the Christmas verse fable she had written for children to which she subsequently gave the title *Keine Stille Nacht* [*Not a silent night*], and it was at once so tender, so humorous, and so wise that I loved it from the very beginning. My enjoyment increased as her reading progressed, and by the time she had finished I knew I had listened to an absolute masterpiece. When Tine asked me to see if I could translate it into English, I felt very doubtful, but when she assured me that a free translation would be acceptable, I agreed to give it a go. After some delay, I started work, and by the beginning of August I had produced a first draft. Since then, Tine has produced, in separate book form, single copies of the two versions of the poem, beautifully illustrated by herself.

It's a great thing that the poem, which has enjoyed a number of popular private readings in both the German original and in my translation, is now, through the backing of John Lucas and Shoestring Press, made more widely available, and given the importance placed within the poem on the value of speaking with other people across the narrow confines of one's native tongue (i.e. of learning other languages), it's highly appropriate that we can now for the first time see the two versions placed side by side in a dual language edition.

I'd like to set down a few remarks about the challenges posed in translating Tine's poem, and how I faced up to them.

There were problems involving the names of characters. Some of these worked well in English—I felt quite happy with Casimir the cat, Rolf the wolf, and even Kunibert the wild boar, but Franz didn't work so well in English as the name of a fox, so he became Rufus, and I felt that the badger-boys might be more English, and less confusing, if they were to become George and Bob rather than Paul and Max. There seemed little point in keeping Isegrim as a proper name for the character we know in English simply as *the big bad wolf.*

Some freedoms were prompted by differences between German and English Christmas delicacies. What should be done with *Mandelsterne, Pfeffernüssen, Butterstollen,* and *Spekulatius*? (Oddly, there was no mention of *lebkuchen* in the original). Almond stars, peppernuts and butterstollen didn't seem right, so I have replaced the German originals with cinnamon, spice, candied peel, walnut whirls, spiced biscuits, mince pies, Yuletide logs, nougat bars and bags of chocolate money without, I hope, jeopardizing anyone's appetite for the poem.

Probably the most important areas where I needed some freedom were cultural—the imperative of Max doing his *Hausaufgaben* in the Christmas holidays, the German folk myth of all the animals being able to understand one anothers' languages on Christmas Eve, and the lines explaining that *Fox* is the English word for *Fuchs*. The last of these examples lent itself to a fairly straightforward substitution, but the first two proved much more difficult. In order to establish, and sustain readers' and listeners' awareness of those cultural factors, I've amplified the original in various places—particularly in the first, second, fifth and seventh sections, and there are references at a couple of points to specific languages (*Rabbitspeak, Squirrelish, Badgerese*) which on this special night have become mutually comprehensible.

Amplification has occurred in places for other reasons as well— the fox's attempted joke about the rabbit and the hedgehog, for example, doesn't really work in English without a joke being told, so I've elaborated a jokey situation not in the original. The description of the raven sitting in the oakwood at the beginning of the third section called out for some more substantial setting of atmosphere than it attracted in the original. The same was true for the description of the festivities in section six, particularly in their closing stages.

One or two small things have been changed for other reasons—
in the seventh section, among a raft of small amplifications,
I've changed the place where Caesar found the fox cub and had
Cleopatra rather than Caesar bestow the name *Vulpecula* on it.
I've also moved the Tacitus reference to the end of that account
rather than have it as an introduction.

What has emerged from these various interventions is a poem
that might better be described as a rendering than as a translation.
The narrative direction and overall structure of the poem are kept,
and I've tried to capture the form, rhythm and rhyme – even the
tone – of the original, all of which I find immensely attractive.
At the same time, I've not held back where I felt that small
embellishments would be in keeping with, and would underpin,
the overall character of the original in an English context. Most
of these are at the level of content—the elaboration of language
components besides vocabulary in section 1, a passing mention of
Basil Brush and the list of vegetables with which the fox has had to
make do before coming upon the rabbit in section 2, Casimir the
cat's embarrassment at mentioning the presence of sugar mice on
the Christmas tree in section 4, the choice of German, Swiss and
Austrian places names and the inclusion of Catalan as a language of
consideration in section 7. I've also, at a stylistic or rhetorical level,
enjoyed incorporating one or two forced rhymes into the poem.

Altogether, the experience of working on Tine's original has been
an immensely enjoyable one, and it is a privilege to be instrumental
in bringing it to the attention and enjoyment of English readers, of
all ages, everywhere.

— *John Gohorry*
*Letchworth Garden City, January 2017*

# KEINE STILLE NACHT

*Und doch eine Weihnachtsgeschichte*

I

Seit Tagen schon hat es geschneit
Und bald, ganz bald ist Weihnachtszeit.
Sehnsuchtsvoll schaut in den Garten
Max und kann es kaum erwarten
Einen Schneemann dort zu bauen
Statt zum Fenster rauszuschauen!
Aber viele Schüler haben,
Wie auch er, noch Hausaufgaben!
Wütend stampft er mit dem Fuß,
Weil er Vokabeln lernen muss.

Zornig und den Tränen nah
Ruft er seinen Großpapa
Und erklärt ihm unumwunden,
Dass er schon seit ein paar Stunden
Hausaufgaben von sich schiebt,
Die er absolut nicht liebt.
Sprachen lernen will er nicht
Zuhause und im Unterricht!
Auch fragt er sich: *weshalb, wozu*
*Er das überhaupt noch tu?*

## NOT A SILENT NIGHT

*A Christmas story with a difference*

I

    Snow's fallen, deep and thick and white
for days and days, and Christmas night
is what Max thinks of, sadly staring
across the gardens he'd like sharing
5    with snowmen, snowballs, skates and slides,
igloos, ice-palaces, ice-rides.
But like most children Max must stay
indoors and not go out to play;
his teachers have all set him work,
10   hard exercise he must not shirk.
School's over, but he'll have no fun
till duty's dusted, homework done.

    Chief of all this is what belongs
to nouns and verbs of foreign tongues,
15   their tenses, cases, genders, moods,
articulations, attitudes,
how they decline or conjugate,
with what words they associate …..
What makes young Max's head so sore?
20   —vocabulary lists galore.
He frets and chafes, he weeps and groans,
he fills the house with plaintive moans;
he calls his Grandad in a huff
*Why must I learn this horrid stuff?*
25   *It gives me headaches, hurts my brain,*
*fills me from ear to ear with pain!*
*To foreign words why pay such heed?*
*plain English ones are all I need.*

Ruhig, ohne Emotion,
Spricht Großpapa zum Enkelsohn:
*Wer Sprachen lernt und sie versteht,*
*Gleich welcher Nationalität,*
*In vielen Ländern Freunde findet,*
*Denn Sprache, lieber Max, verbindet,*
*Und was sie noch bewirken kann,*
*Hör' dir in der Geschichte an,*
*Wie selbst aus Animosität*
*Letztendlich Freundschaft gar entsteht.*

II

Ein schlauer Fuchs mit Namen Franz
Durchstreift mit seinem langen Schwanz
Den Wald, ihm knurrt der Magen,
Gefressen hat er nichts seit Tagen!
Da steht vor einem Tannenbaum,
Der Fuchs traut seinen Augen kaum,
Ein Häschen ohne Angst und Bangen,
Es läuft nicht weg, ist leicht zu fangen!
Der Fuchs leckt gierig mit der Zunge
Sein Maul—schon hebt er an zum Sprunge!
Da schaut der Has' mit festem Blick
Den Gegner an, der weicht zurück!
Und Meister Lampe hebt zum Gruß
Den rechten vord'ren Hasenfuß.
Er schaut ihm furchtlos ins Gesicht
Als er in seiner Sprache spricht:

30    His Grandad takes him by the arm,
his speech is soft, his voice is calm.
*Dear Max,* he says, *whoever knows
a foreign language, when he goes
abroad, can read and understand*
35    *the whys and wherefores of the land;
and he who talks and comprehends
will turn mere strangers into friends.
A foreign language, my dear Max,
halts human folly in its tracks;*
40    *it's hard to scorn, it's hard to hate
when strangers can communicate.
And if you doubt that this is true
here's a wise tale that proves to you
how animosity gives way*
45    *where every speaker has his say.*


II

One night comes stalking through the slush
an ancestor of Basil Brush;
Rufus the fox with chestnut tail,
red, pointed snout and eyes like hail;
50    he hasn't tasted food for weeks
apart from turnips, swedes and leeks,
and these are not what foxes eat;
foxes, you know, survive on meat.
Rufus the fox needs a good dinner;
55    he'll die if he gets any thinner.
He stumbles weakly through the trees,
faints, rises, groans, sinks to his knees;
at last the tree-trunks part, to show
a rabbit playing in the snow!
60    *Now, what a splendid meal is that,
thinks Rufus, chewy, meaty, fat.*

'One night comes stalking through the slush
an ancestor of Basil Brush...'

*Herr Fuchs, es ist die Heil'ge Nacht,*
*Die uns im Wald zu Freunden macht!*
*Gejagt wird heute nirgendwo!*
Da sagt der schlaue Fuchs: *Ach so.*
Verstanden hat er Wort für Wort
Des Hasen Sprache, der fährt fort:
*Ein Wunder ist heut' Nacht geschehn,*
*Wir können alle uns verstehn*
*Und mühelos kommunizieren*
*Die ganze Nacht mit allen Tieren.*


Der Fuchs zeigt sich gesprächsbereit
Und demonstriert Vertraulichkeit,
Leckt zum Beweis die Hasenpfoten,
Die ihm bedenkenlos geboten.




III

Ein Rabe sitzt bei Mondenschein
Auf einem Ast im Eichenhain,

*This rabbit's just the thing for me;
it's breakfast, dinner, lunch and tea!*
He licks his lips, prepares to spring,
65 and then – here's an amazing thing –
the rabbit turns, lifts up a paw,
and says, in Rabbitspeak, *No more!
Dear fox, tonight is Christmas Eve
and predatory habits grieve;*
70 *for friendship's sake, hunting must cease
and we must live tonight in peace!*
The wise old fox has understood
the rabbit's words here in the wood;
he halts, he frowns, steps back a pace
75 and draws conclusions from the case.
*Creatures,* he thinks, *tonight can each
comprehend one another's speech
and language, by some miracle,
tonight creates no obstacle*
80 *to friendship, but the opposite.
Love rules where beasts communicate
and language brings to every species
tonight the priceless gift that peace is.*
He promises to do what's right
85 and to restrain his appetite.

Max looks out at the wintry sky
then sees the warmth in Grandad's eye;
the old man sips weak tea with cream
and then continues with his theme.

III

90 A raven in an oakwood sits
watching the freezing forest. It's
Christmas Eve; the moon's pale light
sends shadows reeling through the night;
strange phantoms rise, and dance, and go
95 like ghosts in some strange magic show.

Als plötzlich er aus seiner Höh'
Ein Lämmchen sieht, so weiß wie Schnee,
Es irrt im Walde schon seit Stunden,
Hat seine Herde nicht gefunden
Und blökt auf jämmerliche Weise!
Da knackt im Unterholz es leise.


Es ist des Fuchsens Duzfreund Rolf,
Der riesengroße graue Wolf.
Er hat das Lamm bereits gewittert,
Das dort vor Angst und Kälte zittert.


Der Wolf nach einer Mahlzeit lechzt!
Ganz aufgeregt der Rabe krächzt:
*Was hast du vor, du störst den Frieden,*
*Der uns in dieser Nacht beschieden!*
*Wir leben heute ohne Not,*
*Sind nicht von Wilderei bedroht!*


Der Wolf heult wütend: *Halt den Schnabel!*
Und Isegrim, so heißt er in der Fabel,
Schleicht sich ans Lamm auf leisen Pfoten.
Der Rabe schreit: *Das ist verboten!*

They loom and fade and swirl their cloaks
then vanish through the mighty oaks.
The raven peers; in this confusion
it's hard to tell fact from illusion,
100 but then among the dark shapes fleeting
he hears a weak, faint, plaintive bleating
and sees, down in the freezing cold,
a snow-white lamb not three months old.
The shepherd's put his flock to bed
105 but missed  this little sleepy-head
who's hungry, stranded, frightened, weak,
and scared of shadows dare not speak.
The sharp-eared raven hears the sound
of small twigs snapping on the ground;
110 it's Rufus Fox's good friend Rolf,
the fierce, grey, hungry, big bad wolf.
The lamb bleats like a beast demented;
the wolf already has him scented;
he bares his teeth and licks his paws,
115 saliva rains down from his jaws.
It stains the snow with yellow drops
as Rolf imagines fresh lamb chops.
He crouches low behind the stump
of a dead tree and waits to jump.
120 The bird, incensed at what he sees,
upbraids the wolf in words like these;
*What is your plan? What's your agenda?*
*A wolf should be a lamb's defender.*
*You stir up trouble, breach the peace,*
125 *heap terror on a snow-white fleece.*
*Tonight's the one night of the year*
*when creatures should live free of fear.*
*Freedom is not as you supposed;*
*tonight, the hunting season's closed!*
130 The angry wolf howls *Shut your beak,*
*old raven! Who asked you to speak?*
then rushes out from where he's hidden.
The raven cries out *That's forbidden!*

'the wolf already has him scented;
he bares his teeth and licks his paws,
saliva rains down from his jaws...'

Mit lautem Krächzen er betont:
*Das zarte Lämmchen bleibt verschont!*
*Es mangelt, Meister Isegrim,*
*Dir offensichtlich an Benimm!*
Da wird der graue Wolf verlegen
Und murmelt leise: *Meinetwegen.*
Auch die Geschichte endet gut,
Wenngleich nach heftigem Disput!


IV


Die Maus verschläft normalerweis'
Den Winter unter Schnee und Eis.
Doch nirgends wird in dieser Nacht
An Winterschlaf auch nur gedacht!
Und voller Neugier hüpft die Maus
Aus ihrem Erdloch flink heraus.
Sie landet dicht vor Kasimir,
Dem Kater aus dem Forstrevier.
Der weiß zwar, dass die Mäusejagd
Ist strengstens heute untersagt!
Doch weil das Mäuschen gar nicht flieht,
Denkt er bei sich: *Wenn's keiner sieht ...*
*Und niemand merkt, dann fang ich dich,*
*Ein Katzensprung nur ist's für mich!*
Mit seiner Pfote blitzesschnell

He shouts and croaks without respite,
135 his harsh voice echoes through the night,
he croaks and shouts without reserve
*This tender lamb you must preserve.*
*You big bad wolf. It's plain to see*
*manners and wolves just don't agree.*
140 *Conduct like yours is not admired;*
*it leaves a lot to be desired.*
*Keep off, vamoose, get out of range,*
*and learn some manners, for a change.*
The wolf, embarrassed, sees what's just
145 and slinks off, growling *If I must.*


IV

*Two cases now,* says thoughtful Max,
*where talk halts predators' attacks.*
His granddad sips warm milk and rum;
*Indeed,* he says, *and more's to come.*

Mice usually sleep safe and sound
150 throughout the winter underground
but one small mouse does not believe
in sleep at all on Christmas Eve;
inquisitive, he jumps and hops
then nimbly from his hole he pops.
155 In front of whom does he appear?
the forest tomcat, Casimir,
who knows full well that hunting mice
tonight's outlawed at any price.
But all the same, he's strongly tempted
160 —there's nothing really to prevent it;
the mouse makes no attempt to flee;
it's late, it's dark; no-one will see.
If no-one sees, that's good enough!

'Like lightning he whips out his claws
and pins the poor mouse in his paws.'

Berührt er Mäuschens weiches Fell!
Erschrocken fasst es sich ans Herz!

Da schnurrt der Kater: *War nur 'n Scherz,*
*Schau, Kleines, in die Augen mir,*
*Ein Schmusekater steht vor dir!*
*Wir wollen uns die Pfoten reichen!*
Die Maus schlägt ein—mit Fragezeichen,
Denn Kater sind, das ist erwiesen,
Für sie mit Vorsicht zu genießen.

Drum sagt sie sich: *Man weiß ja nie...*
Doch langsam fasst Vertrauen sie
Und ist beruhigt, da zumal
Der Kater gibt sich jovial.

*Und nun,* schnurrt Kater Kasimir,
*Verrat' ich ein Geheimnis dir!*

*Vom Igel hörte ich die Kunde,*
*Dass eine Botschaft macht die Runde:*
*Im Wald, inmitten einer Lichtung,*
*Beschrieben hat er mir die Richtung,*
*Steht immer in der Weihnachtszeit*
*Ein Tannenbaum für uns bereit,*
*Er ist geschmückt, nicht zu vergessen,*
*Mit köstlichen Delikatessen.*
*Und wer im Wald ist aufgewacht,*

165   he's only a cat's whisker off.
      Like lightning he whips out his claws
      and pins the poor mouse in his paws.
      The little mouse emits a squeak;
      to save his life he cannot speak
170   but just in time, the cat recalls
      tonight's imperative, and stalls.
      *My tiny, timid friend,* he purrs,
      *this was a poor joke, nothing worse.*
      *Look deep into my sea-green eyes;*
175   *a kindly cat before you lies.*
      *Let us shake paws—I'll make amends*
      *and surely we two can be friends.*
      The mouse complies—with some reserve,
      for cats, as is well known, deserve
180   to be approached with care and tact
      by humble mice, and that's a fact.
      He thinks *With cats, one never knows*
      *which way the wind is, how it blows.*
      But this cat seems kind, well-intentioned,
185   and peace can thrive where friendship's mentioned.
      Their paws touch; then cat Casimir
      bends closer to the mouse's ear.
      *Listen,* he purrs, *and I'll reveal*
      *secrets a true friend can't conceal.*
190   The mouse, still feeling rather pale,
      sits up and listens to his tale.

      *A spiky hedgehog,* says the cat
      *talked in the wood of this and that;*
      *each year, he tells me, as it's nearing*
195   *cold Christmas Eve, he finds a clearing*
      *here in the wood where there's a pine*
      *its branches decked with ribbons fine*
      *and in these ribbons, pretty parcels*
      *jam-packed with most delicious morsels,*
200   *small snacks and nibbles, titbits sweet*

*Der pilgert in der Heiligen Nacht*
*Zur Stelle, wo der Christbaum steht.*
*Mach' dich bereit, eh' es zu spät.*
*Auch unterwegs sind Paul und Max.*
*Die Buben der Familie Dachs.*
*Komm' mit zum großen Festtagsschmaus!*
*Sagt Kasimir und geht voraus.*


*Die Maus, noch etwas zögerlich,*
*Ruft plötzlich: Warte doch auf mich!*
*Gibt's Mandelsterne dort mit Zimt?*
*Darauf der Kater: Ganz bestimmt!*
*Jetzt kennt die Maus kein Halten mehr,*
*Sie läuft dem Kater hinterher,*
*Der sich soeben aufgemacht*
*Zum Weihnachtsbaum in dunkler Nacht.*
*Und weil das Mäuschen ist so klein,*
*Legt es sogleich ein Päuschen ein*
*Und kuschelt sich auf Katers Rücken.*
*Lauscht seinem Schnurren mit Entzücken.*


*'The mouse no longer hesitates*
*but down the path accelerates*
*to Casimir, who bends his back...'*

*for all the animals to eat.*
*There are all kinds of nice confections;*
*the hedgehog gave precise directions.*
*Hush! Can you hear that laughing noise?*
205 *It's George and Bob, the badger boys*
*already heading for the feast;*
*they must be halfway there, at least.*
He preens his whiskers, pats his nose
then off into the wood he goes
210 towards the festive Christmas tree.
The mouse shouts to him *Wait for me!*
*Will there be cinnamon and spice?*
*Yes!* says the cat, *and sugar mice!*
then blushes at what mouse might feel
215 *I meant to say—and candied peel.*
The mouse no longer hesitates
but down the path accelerates
to Casimir, who bends his back
and plucks him swiftly from the track;
220 he snuggles down deep in his fur
and listens to the tomcat purr.

V

Am Weihnachtsbaume kommt sodann
Ein Tier nach dem andern an.

Der Igel ist schon da, wie stets,
Begrüßt den Hasen: *Na, wie geht's?*
Der, seinerseits, entgegnet heiter:
*Gruß an die Frau!* und hoppelt weiter.
Für jeden gibt es Leckerbissen,
Es riecht nach Zimt und Pfeffernüssen,
Nach Äpfeln und nach Zuckerwatte,
Dem Leibgericht der Wanderratte.
Und durch den tief verschneiten Tann
Stolziert das Ehepaar Fasan
Zum weihnachtlichen Stelldichein.
Trifft auf ein Eichhorn, das allein
Schon mehrmals war an Ort und Stelle,
Und es erzählt, dass es für alle Fälle
Vorsorglich hier vergraben müsse
Säcke voller Haselnüsse,
Mandeln, Makadamia,
Krokantgebäck et cetera.

Auf einem Baumstumpf steht sogar
Ein Topf mit echtem Kaviar.
Der Wolf, er schnüffelt zwar daran,

## V

    The animals come, one, two, three,
    to join each other round the tree.
    Now through the forest deep in snow
225 a pair of stately pheasants go
    with strutting steps, as pheasants do,
    to keep the Christmas rendez-vous.
    The clearing's loud with conversation;
    the owl's deep hoot needs no translation,
230 and Squirrelish or Badgerese
    are understood by all with ease.
    Hedgehog's already up and doing
    and asks the rabbit *How's it going?*
    Courtesy's what the rabbit likes;
235 *Not bad! Yourself? And Mrs Spikes?*
    A heavy branch looms overhead;
    it's weighted down with gingerbread,
    candyfloss, apples red and white,
    the brown rat's table-top delight,
240 and by its trunk the dormouse girls
    are playing catch with walnut whirls.
    The wild boar Kunibert has found
    sweet satisfaction by the pound;
    his snout's ecstatic as he hogs
245 truffles, spiced biscuits, Yuletide logs.
    His appetite is not in question;
    he has no fear of indigestion.
    A small cat with her tiny feet
    holds Christmas cookies, sugar-sweet.
250 Don't think those chocolate hoops will last;
    woodpeckers' beaks work very fast!
    The lamb and raven both partake
    of cold mince pies and almond cake,
    while on a tree-stump stands a jar
255 heaped to the brim with caviar.
    The wolf sniffs round it, as wolves can,

'And now the party's in full flow...'

*'The night speeds swiftly on its way
to moonset, twilight, break of day
with stories, laughter, jokes and mirth,
sweet recreations of the earth.'*

Doch lieber mag er Marzipan.
Auch Kunibert, das wilde Schwein,
Stellt pünktlich sich am Treffpunkt ein,
Schmatzt grunzend und mit Hochgenuss
Am liebsten Spekulatius.
Und während alle schnabulieren,
Genüsslich Leckeres goutieren,
Verschränkt der graue Wolf die Pfoten,
Erzählt dem Wildschwein Anekdoten.

Die Eule hat erstaunt vernommen,
Dass ihr der Kauz zuvorgekommen!
Der habe sich, ganz ungeniert,
Die Zuckermäuschen reserviert!
Der Kauz sei unverhältnismäßig
Gierig, maßlos und gefräßig!
So ein Benehmen ist wahrscheinlich
Der weisen Eule äußerst peinlich;
Drum breitet sie die Flügel aus,
Schwebt lautlos durch die Nacht nach Haus.
Ein Kätzchen hält in seinen Tätzchen
Zuckersüße Weihnachtsplätzchen.
Siebenschläferkinder scherzen
Und spielen Ball mit Schokoherzen,
Der Rabe und das Lämmchen wollen
Nichts anderes als Butterstollen.
Fast alle Schokoladenkringel
Stibitzt der Buntspecht, dieser Schlingel!

VI

Dann stellt der Fuchs die Ohren spitz:
*Kennt ihr den allerneu'sten Witz*
*Vom Hasen und vom Igeltier?*
Sein Freund winkt ab: *Den kennen wir!*
Ein wenig ist der Fuchs gekränkt,

but best of all likes marzipan;
he sits cross-legged against a fence
260  filled full of vulpine eloquence
and while the others fill their throats
regales the boar with anecdotes.

VI

And now the party's in full flow.
285  *Does anyone,* the fox asks, *know
the joke about the urchin rabbit
who grew up with a hedgehog's habit
of rolling up into a ball*

Weil keiner ihm Beachtung schenkt,
Bleibt aber friedlich und gemütlich,
Tut sich am Schweizer Käse gütlich.


Es wird gescherzt, es wird gelacht
Und viel erzählt in dieser Nacht,
Der Fuchs bringt seiner lieben Frau
Gebrannte Mandeln in den Bau.


Den Kindern, die daheimgeblieben,
Packt Kunibert, für alle sieben
Weihnachtsbäckereien ein
Und Honigkuchen obendrein.

*and couldn't then uncurl at all?*
290  *Yes!* shout his friends, *but prejudice
has no place on a night like this.*
The fox turns sulky, quite upset
his sense of humour's so ill-met
but promptly expiates his guilt on
295  a plate heaped high with fine old Stilton.

The night speeds swiftly on its way
to moonset, twilight, break of day
with stories, laughter, jokes and mirth,
sweet recreations of the earth.
300  The time of parting comes too soon
as the last vestige of the moon
slips from the sky and, in the east,
sunrise illuminates the feast.

From far away, a nightingale
305  charms the whole clearing with her tale;
softly the raven, lamb and boar
add their small music to her store;
the cat and mouse, too, add a voice,
and bid the brand-new day rejoice.
310  Song wells up from the rabbit's throat;
the hedgehog hums a fine bass note.
Only the grey wolf, out of key,
bawls tone-deaf discords, raucously.

For those who could not come tonight
315  a little something's wrapped up tight
—cakes for the raven's nest, and then
burnt almonds for the foxes' den.
For his enormous wild boar brood
Kunibert stacks up piles of food
320  —seven Christmas pastries thick with honey,
nougat bars, bags of chocolate money.

Den Kaviar, den er nicht mag,
Schenkt Isegrim am nächsten Tag
Der alten Wölfin mit dem Satz:
*Für dich verzicht' ich gern, mein Schatz!*

VII

Vorbei ist nun die Heil'ge Nacht,
Die ringsum Freude hat gebracht,
Die friedlich, ohne Streiterei
Und Angst und Schrecken ging vorbei!
Denn dank der Sprache hat für Stunden
Ein Miteinander statt gefunden.
Dem Wolf wird es ums Herze warm,
Nimmt jeden noch in seinen Arm
Und ruft dann im Nachhausegehn:
*Bis nächstes Jahr, auf Wiedersehn!*


Jetzt lacht der Max und macht sich dann
Vergnügt ans Wörterlernen dran!


In England und Amerika,
In Irland und in Kanada
Sowie im ganzen Schottenland
Wird unser Rotfuchs *fox* genannt.
Bei jedem Wetter, selbst bei Sturm,
Schleicht in der Nacht zum Eiffelturm
in Frankreichs Hauptstadt *le renard,*
In Spanien heisst er *zorro* gar,
Λuca in Petersburg und Minsk,
In Moskau und in Tscheljabinsk,
Selbst dort, wo eisige Kälte droht,
Im fernen Nischnij-Nowgorod.

The wolf brings for his old wife, Nancy,
the caviar he doesn't fancy.
*It's yours,* he says, *and it's a pleasure*
*to give things up for you, my treasure.*

VII

Now, at last, Christmas Eve has gone
and the festivities are done,
enjoyed in peace, without dissent,
fear, conflict, terror, argument.
The wolf's cold heart at last is warm;
he hugs the others, arm in arm
and calls out to them when they leave
*Goodbye until next Christmas Eve!*

Now Max is happy, and has fun
with atlas, word-list, lexicon
enthusiastic, animated,
to find out how *Fox* is translated.
In Thun and by the Bodensee,
Vienna, Stuttgart, Linz, Saas-Fee,
in Hameln, Zurich, and again
in Hannover, near Wennigsen,
everywhere – on the street, in books –
the German word for *Fox* is *Fuchs*.
In gay Paris, in shine or rain,
where fly-boats cruise the river Seine
ask who comes prowling from afar.
It is the hunter, *Le renard*.
In Spain, where girls bring wine in jars
as midnight pulses with guitars,

*La volpe* dreht zu später Stunde
Ums Kolosseum eine Runde.
In der Antike schreckte wohl
Die Gänse auf dem Kapitol
Manch *vulpes*, wenn er hatte Lust
Auf Gänseklein, sowie auf Brust.
Die Vögel aber, mit Gezeter,
Vertrieben laut den Übeltäter!
Sie schlugen einst, das ist verbucht,
Sogar die Gallier in die Flucht!

Bei Tacitus ist nachzulesen.
Wer weiß, ob's wirklich so gewesen,

Dass Cäsar einst am Wegesrand
Ein winzig kleines Füchslein fand.
Das schenkte er Kleopatra
Und nannte es *vulpecula*.
Wer das nicht glauben mag, der such'
Das Füchselein im Wörterbuch!

a cow is *vaca*, bull is *toro*
and Mr Fox's name is *Zorro*.
But if from Santiago's doors
355   you trail him east through paradors
at Barcelona you must stop.
In Catalan, a fox is *llop*.
In Omsk, Tomsk, Moscow, Chelyabinsk,
a fox is *lusa*, and in Minsk.
360   The same applies, whoever goes
to Krasnojarsk's Siberian snows.
In Rome at night *La Volpe* rounds
the Coliseum's ruined grounds;
in ancient times, the geese who sat in
365   the Capitol cried out (in Latin)
*Vulpes!* when fox came on the loose
for grey-lag giblets, breast of goose.
The birds, aroused in wild disorder,
scared off the bushy-tailed marauder
370   and once, books say, achieved the feat
of driving Gaul's troops to defeat.



Great Caesar found a baby fox
375   beside the Tiber in the rocks
and gave the cub, pale, gaunt and lean,
to Cleopatra, Egypt's queen.
She brought it up in royal style
and took it with her on the Nile.
380   Her care for it was most particular;
she called it her beloved *Vulpecula*.
Whoever doubts it happened thus
can read it all in Tacitus.

VIII

Nun aber ist für heute Schluss,
Und Großpapa kriegt einen Kuss!

## VIII

*That's all for now,* Grandad declares,
385  *bed's waiting for you up the stairs.*
Max, sleepy, answers *Thanks for this*
and gives Grandad a goodnight kiss.

BIOGRAPHICAL NOTES

John Gohorry was born Donald Smith in Coventry, UK, in 1943. He spent the 1960s at the University of London, obtaining an M.Phil. there in 1970. He lectured in Further/Higher Education until retirement in 2006. He has published nine collections of poems, most recently *The Age of Saturn* (Shoestring 2015) and *Impromptus for George Erdmann, with The Good Samaritan, a libretto for a Conjectural Abendmusik 1705* (Lapwing, 2015). His sequence *Thirty Three Ostrich Cadenzas* appeared from Shoestring earlier this year.

Previous collections include *Adagios on Ré/Adagios en Ré* (Lapwing, 2014), a sequence of 79 short poems written over three years on the Ile de Ré, with accompanying French translations by the author, *Samuel Johnson's Amber* (Shoestring Press, 2010), and two sets of poems engaging with Zen koans, *Forty Eight Gates* and *On the Blue Cliff* (Dark Age Press, 2009 and 2012 respectively). His poem 'Lost' won the 2008 Keats/Shelley Memorial Association Poetry Competition.

He is Poet in Residence at David's Bookshop, Letchworth Garden City.

\*

Bettine Koch (geb. Schmid) wurde 1942 in Stuttgart geboren und hat nach dem Schauspielstudium einige Jahre an verschiedenen Bühnen gespielt. Ihr ständiger Wohnsitz ist Stuttgart wo sie geheiratet hat und wo ihre fünf Kinder geboren wurden. Neben Literatur und Kunst ist die Musik ihre Lieblingsbeschäftigung. Sie spielt und unterrichtet Klavier. Der Wunsch ihrer Kinder war schon immer ein eigenes für sie geschriebenes Buch.